Martin the Mouse

My Dad is a pilot.
He flies a fine big jet plane.
He loves flying.
Martin is my pet mouse.
He will eat anything.
He is only a little mouse, but he loves flying, too!

Sometimes Martin goes flying with my Dad.
I will tell you why.

Martin lives in a little cage.
One day, he got out.
He found an old mouse-hole.
He hid in it.

I looked and looked,
but I could not find
my little friend.
I was very sad.
The cat will catch him,
I thought.

When we went to bed,
Martin came out.
He found some jam.
He ate some.
It got all over his
little feet.
Soon there was jam
all over the carpet.

He found the ink.
He put his feet in it.
Then there was ink
on the carpet, too.
Martin was having
a fine time!

Then he found some glue.
He just had to try it.
So he knocked it over.
What a mess!
There was jam and ink
and glue all over the carpet!

Martin sat down to wash.
He sat on a warm black rug.
Suddenly the rug got up.
It was Blacky, the cat!

Martin ran.
He could not
find his mouse-hole.
He could not
get to his cage.
So he ran up the curtains.

The window was open a little.
Martin jumped out.
He thought he was safe.
Blacky could not get
out of the window.
It was very dark.
It was very cold.

Now Martin could hear lots of cats singing in the garden.

They were singing about the mice they would catch.

They were singing about the mice they would eat.

Martin was frightened.

He wished he was back in his safe warm cage.

Suddenly he saw two big eyes in the dark.

Then two more big eyes.
The cats were coming!
Martin ran up the garden.
He ran for his life.
But the cats were catching him up.
What could he do?

He got to the garage.
It was shut.
But there was a little hole in the door.
Martin jumped through.
He was safe again.
Martin was tired.
He wanted a safe place to sleep.

He ran round the car.
The doors were shut.
But the boot was open.

Martin climbed inside.
He found a little case.
The top was open.

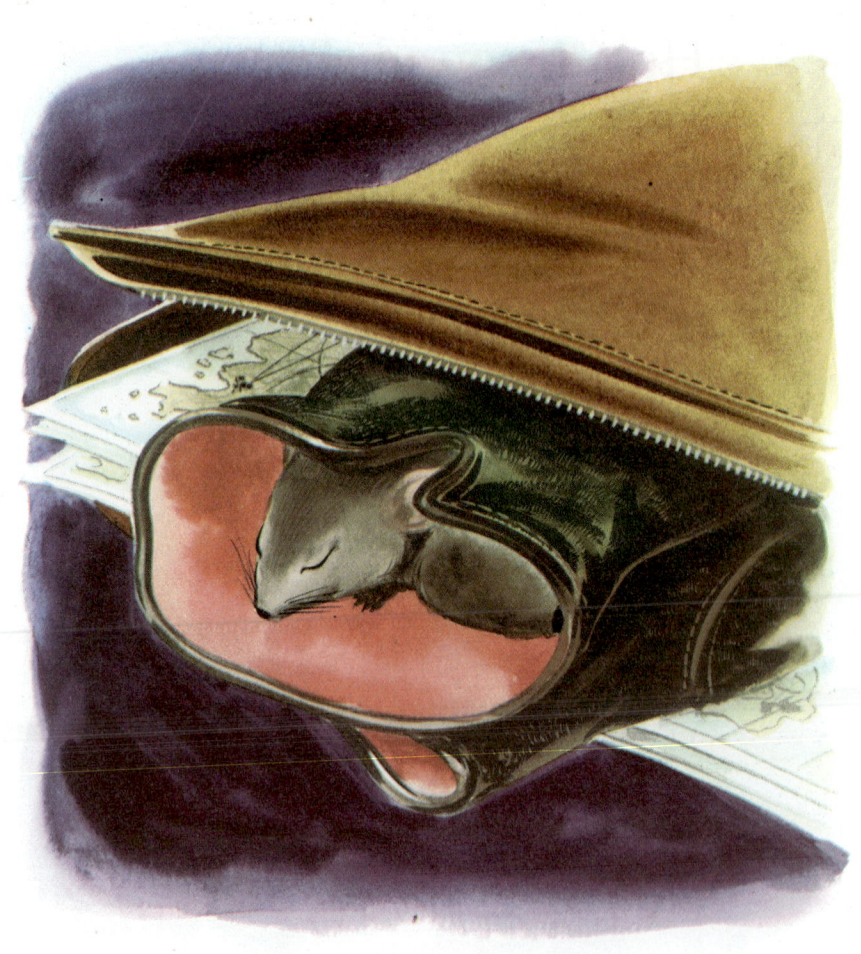

Inside there were maps,
and two warm gloves.
Martin crept into one.
Soon he was fast asleep.

Martin woke up.

His safe warm hiding place was going up and down.

He tried to get out, but the case was shut now.

Martin was frightened.

He was only a little mouse.

He did not know it was morning.

He did not know my Dad was driving to the airport.

He did not know my Dad had to fly to London!

My Dad parked the car at the airport.

He opened the boot and took out his case.

"I must not forget that," he said to himself.

He did not know who was inside!

My Dad got into the jet plane.

He put his case on a rack.

The passengers got in.

The second pilot started the engines.

It was time to take off.

Then the air hostess came into the cockpit.

"Ready for take-off, sir," she said.

My Dad looked at her.

"I do not think I know you," he said.

"Where is Miss Williams? She is our air hostess today."

"Miss Williams is ill," said the girl.
"I am Miss Jones.
I had to take her place,"

"Right, Miss Jones," said my Dad.
"We are taking off now."

Soon the plane was climbing through the clouds.

"Pass my gloves, please," said my Dad.
"They are in my case."

The second pilot opened the case.

He put his hand inside. Then he jumped.

"There is a little mouse in your case," he said.

"A mouse? How did that get there?" said my Dad.

"Take over, and I will have a look."

"Quick!" said the second pilot.

"It has got out. Catch it!"

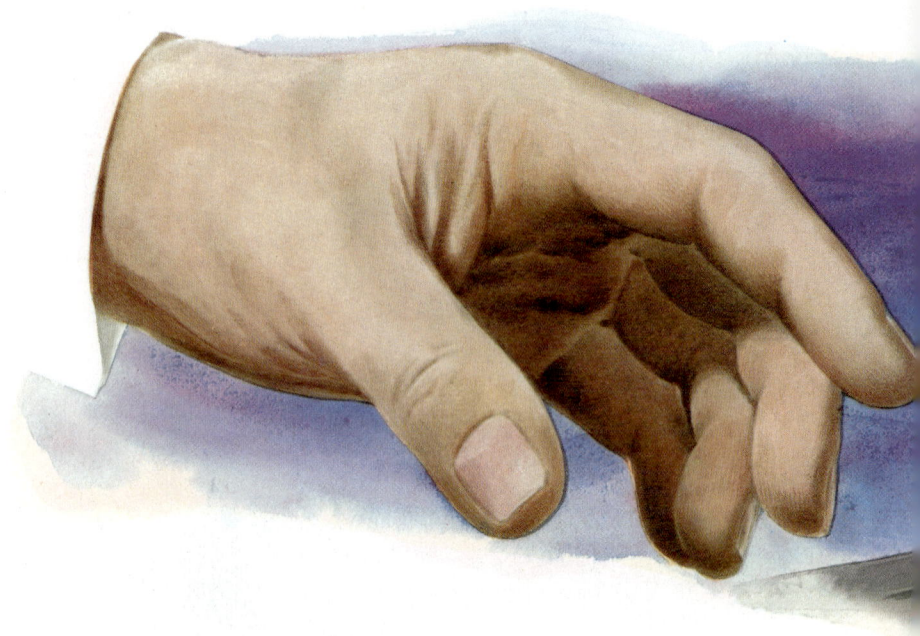

Then Martin had fun.
He ran round the cockpit.
He jumped on the seats.
He climbed up some wires.
He liked this funny
little room, full of good
smells.
He started to eat
a rubber mat.

"Got you!"

He picked Martin up.

Then he saw Martin's little feet.

They were black and red with ink and jam.

They had glue on them.

"Martin!" said my Dad.
"So that is where you were hiding.
You bad mouse.
What a mess you made of our carpet!"
"This is our pet mouse," he said to the second pilot. "We lost him."

"He wants something to eat," said the second pilot. "I will give him some chocolate.

Let him run about for a bit.

I think he likes flying."

So Martin had a fine time.
He ate the chocolate.
He played in the cockpit.
He sat on the second pilot's arm and looked out.
Then he sniffed at the mat.
He started to eat it again.

"Here," said my Dad,
"you cannot eat that."

He picked Martin up and put him back in the case.
"That mouse will eat anything," said my Dad.
"He must stay in my case."

"Mike, November," said the radio.

"Mike, November. Go ahead," said my Dad.

"Mike, November," said the radio.

"Miss Williams has been found bound and gagged.

Take care!

Your air hostess is a *spy*.

Police will meet you at London Airport.

Over."

"Do not answer," said a voice.

"Do not turn round. I have a gun."

It was the air hostess!
She had come back
to the cockpit.
She had heard the radio.
"You are not an air hostess at all," said my Dad.
"You are a spy!"

"Yes," said the spy. "But no one will catch me now."

"Mike, November," said the radio.

"Can you hear me?
Are you all right?
Come in, please."

"Turn off the radio," said the spy.

"Turn the plane round.
If there are police at London, we will go to Paris."

The second pilot turned for Paris.
He had to.

"You will not get away,"
he said.
"I have friends
in Paris," answered the spy.
"They will see I get away."

My Dad was thinking hard.

He had to get hold of that gun.

But what could he do?
Then he had an idea.
"You have no maps," he said.
"You cannot get away without maps."

The spy smiled.

"Then I will have your maps," she said.

She stuck the gun in my Dad's back.

"Where are they?"

"In my case," said my Dad.

Women were frightened of mice, he thought.

If only Martin makes her jump I will get that gun.

The spy got the case.

She opened it with one hand.

She felt inside.

My Dad got ready.

The second pilot got ready, too.

He knew what my Dad was thinking.

Martin put his head out.

He could smell things to eat.

Suddenly he shot up the spy's arm!

My Dad moved.

"Get back!" said the spy.

She put Martin on the floor.

"That was a silly trick. Did you think a little mouse would frighten a spy?"

She got out the maps.
"I will have these," she said.
"Now fly to Paris. No more tricks, or I shoot."
The plane flew on and on.
Now my Dad was very worried.

His chance had gone.

No one knew the plane was going to Paris.

No one could help them.

My Dad's plane was in real trouble.

But what could he do?

He looked down.

Martin was having a fine time.

He was playing by the radio.

He was not worried.

He did not know the plane was in trouble.

He was only a little mouse.

Now they were getting near Paris.

The second pilot was worried.

He was thinking hard, too.

He said, "I must turn on the radio.

I must ask if I can land."

"No," said the spy.

"You do not catch me like that."

The second pilot turned on his landing lights.

"Turn those lights off," said the spy.

"You can land without lights.

The runway has lights."

"It is not safe to land without lights," said my Dad.

"It is not safe to land without the radio.

Another plane may run into us. We may crash."

"You will land now. Without radio and without lights," said the spy.

She waved the gun.

"If you do not land I will shoot."

We will crash, thought my Dad.

I have got to get that gun.

But how?

The second pilot put the wheels down.

Then he sniffed.

"Something is burning," he said.

My Dad looked down. Smoke was coming from the radio.

"We are on fire!" he shouted.

"Quick!
Give me the fire extinguisher.
It is by my case."

Now the spy looked frightened.

She gave the fire extinguisher to my Dad.

"Put it out! Put it out!" she shouted. The smoke was getting worse.

My Dad pointed the
fire extinguisher down.
A jet of foam shot out.
But it did not hit the fire.
It hit the spy in the face!

My Dad was holding the fire extinguisher upside-down!

The spy dropped the gun.

"I cannot see!" she shouted.

But now my Dad had the gun.

He passed the fire extinguisher to the second pilot.

Foam went everywhere.

"Get that fire out," he said.

"Do not land.

We have plenty of fuel.

We will get our passengers to London yet.

We will take our air hostess there, too.

The police will be pleased to see her."

My Dad tied the spy up.
She looked a mess.
A real mess!

He told the passengers what had happened.

Then he saw Martin.

He was covered with foam.

He was a mess too!

"Poor little mouse," said my Dad.
"What a time you have had!"

He picked Martin up.
He wiped the little mouse.
Martin felt better.
He sat on my Dad's shoulder and looked out.
He was happy again.

The plane landed at London Airport.
Police took the spy away.
They said my Dad was a hero.

He had to go to the police station.

Then they drove him all the way home in a big police car.

Martin went too.

He thought it was fine fun!

Later my Dad told me what had happened.
   I was so proud of him.
He was a hero!
   I was so happy that Martin was safe too.

He was a bad little mouse, but he was my friend.

"You bad little mouse," I said.

"He is not a bad little mouse," said my Dad.

"He is a fine little friend."

I did not understand.

"Martin ate the rubber on the radio wires," said my Dad.

"Then they got hot and smoked.

I could not have saved the plane without him."

"Oh, Martin," I said.
"You are a hero too!"
I stroked my little friend and gave him some cheese.

He was only a little mouse, but he had helped to save a jet plane.

He had helped to catch a spy!

So that is why Martin the Mouse goes flying with my Dad.
    They are both heroes.
Martin loves flying.
He loves to see what is going on in the cockpit.

But now he has to stay in a cage.

Sometimes he wonders why.

There are so many things that smell good to eat in a jet plane!